From heavenly Father to me to You

by
Yovonne Jenkins

Gotham Books

30 N Gould St.
Ste. 20820, Sheridan, WY 82801
https://gothambooksinc.com/

Phone: 1 (307) 464-7800

Published by Gotham Books (July 19, 2022)

ISBN: 978-1-956349-98-6 (sc)
ISBN: 978-1-956349-99-3 (e)

Because of the dynamic nature of the Internet, any web addresses or links contained in this book may have changed since publication and may no longer be valid.

The views expressed in this work are solely those of the author and do not necessarily reflect the views of the publisher, and the publisher hereby disclaims any responsibility for them

TABELE OF CONTENTS

Yovonne O Jenkins was born in 1951 at Ft. Hood, TX, the first of four children. They learned to be flexible at an early age as a cross-country move could come at any time. As the eldest of two bothers and a sister, Yovonne took responsibility for upholding her parent's standards when they were away, much to the dismay of her siblings.

Yovonne learned to quickly earn the trust of neighbors and schoolmates during her multiple relocations. As with many children who grow up everywhere, she learned that shyness seldom gets a person anywhere. She developed an outgoing style based upon honesty and kindness which has served her well throughout her life. She makes lasting friends wherever she goes. She breaks down barriers by sharing her life's lessons with others in a quest to help them avoid the pitfalls and painful detours that attract the unwary. She loves learning and believes the greatest success in life is self-mastery.

Yovonne's creative side includes drawing, painting, reading and writing poetry. As a teenager, she became engrossed in mystery novels and devoured books about scientific anomalies and space travel. She then graduated to biographies and was intrigued by perspectives on life presented in them. She realized that an individual's unique experience shapes her view and affects the way she understands others. While a painting or sculpture will never be more than the finished product, a person is never finished until she becomes the image of God; of Love. Yovonne maintains a spirit of gratitude through the joys and sorrows of life and seeks to inspire the good in fellow travelers she encounters on the road of life.

Yovonne again proves that life can be wonderful if we follow the great commandment to "Love one another" and to serve those we meet in our own unique way.

This week I have been pondering the change of heart Alma was talking about in the scriptures. I believe as we feast upon God's Word we become filled with light and the desire to do good. The thought came to me feasting is like dining on your favorite foods... how you love that extra whip cream on the top of your strawberry shortcake, and maybe a drizzle of chocolate or maple. It is something you look forward to often and fills you with joy and great anticipation. What if our partaking of the scriptures was that delightful? In 2 Nephi 32:3 we read: 3Angels speak by the power of the Holy Ghost; wherefore, they speak the words of Christ. Wherefore, I said unto you, feast upon the words of Christ; for behold, the words of Christ will tell you all things what ye should do. 1 John 4:7-8 reads Beloved, let us love one another for love is from God and whoever loves has been born of God and know God. Anyone who does not love does not know God because God is love.... so, to love is to know God, and to know God is everything. So, charity is love. May we each seek to be filled with this love that we may be prepared in all things.

Foreword

This work has been created to touch
every "ounce" of you ... your senses,
thoughts and spirit (i.e. mind, body and soul).
Via a loving Father from which all beauty,
love and joy originates.
He has seen fit to use me to deliver this gift to you.
So please feast upon the beauty of it.

Dedication

March 3, 1931 – December 10, 1990

To Mother, who always enjoyed my artwork
(no matter how hideous it was!!).
And was an exceptional example of love unconditional;
Through her gift
I was blessed too diligently
"seek the Giver of all perfect gifts"!
For that I am eternally grateful.
May this collection of artwork and prose uplift and edify the body,
mind and spirit.
Giving all glory and honor to the giver
of all good gifts. And expressing gratitude for the
opportunity to be "an instrument in His hands"

Jesus Christ is the Way
Walk therein
And ye shall find love
unconditional; joy eternal
And peace within your very soul.

Forgiveness is an unusual thing
For as we exercise it towards others
We are then healed of our pains and inadequacies
How excellent art thou oh Lord, in all thy ways
That through obedience to thee we are made whole!!!

What If

What if we are sons and daughters of God, given physical bodies to live here on earth? That while here we should experience good and evil; that we might chose good over evil. What if when we chose good our heavenly Father rewards us; in His own way? Giving some material comfort, others mental well-being, others health, others the ability to see beyond this physical plane, and so on. What if when we chose evil over good Father allows us not to reap sudden punishment; but gives us opportunities to see the err of our ways and repent?

What if God asked us to pray to Him as "Our Father", because families are of uttermost importance to Him? And because they are so He has given us a way for our family unit to remain intact eternally.

What if God really does exist and loves us and desires us to love Him? And what if all we had to do to except His love was to acknowledge that we are all imperfect (sinners); unable to permanently correct our sinful nature on our own; that we are in need of saving (salvation). Then we could except; by faith His perfect plan of salvation for our lives!!! Faith in the Lord Jesus Christ; acknowledging that Jesus Christ is the only begotten Son of God. What if we prayed for an understanding of these things--- received an acknowledgment of the truth of them and never acted upon that knowledge? Wouldn't it be disappointing? To have had the opportunity to have "heaven" and never endeavored to see if it might be attainable? What if this life really is a "test"—a preparatory state for eternity? Not only for you; but for you and the ones you love?

PRIDE

Pride robs
The ones you love
of the blessings they
could receive in service to you
It denies them the joy that comes from
being used by our heavenly Father's hand
Destroys trust; for that is what is required
for us to share our burdens and trials.
Strange how we can give service and receive the many blessings
thereof--- And the joy therein
But deny our loved ones the same privilege;
even our husbands and/or wives, children and/or parents—

Even
Jesus, our Savior
and heavenly Father.

Power

It is the ability to control oneself;
in the most irritating of circumstances
The ability to act;
not just react
To set the standard; not just live it
It comes from within and
transcends all that is without
It disciplines itself, thereby
bringing even the cosmos
under its dominion
It reigns in love and truth and lives
one standard for all;
Thus is constantly in tune with
heavenly Father's will
It is the "Golden Rule" manifested!

EVIL

Those of color swear it is "white"
And those who are not of color say it's black
What both fail to see is
that it does not discriminate or pre-judge.
It is an equal opportunity corrupter; "it is ... like a
roaring lion... seeking whom he may devour"
Since things are seldom as they appear, we must take
care not to label or judge each other; For in so doing we
become pawns of the devourer--
And our paths become the road to destruction.
And what is accomplished ---
since black and white are not colors;
but statuses of light!
MUST WE CONTINUE IN IGNORANCE AND RUDE;
UNCHRISTLIKE BEHAVIOR ?!?
Can't we remember that beauty comes in all shapes,
sizes and colors ---
Does not come from without but from within;
Where only God can see.
So our position as children of God is not to judge;
for all must stand before the same seat of judgment
And all shall be judged by the same Lord, Savior
and Creator Only He sees all and knows all---
Therefore only He knows for sure
who is who and what is what

LOVING

What brings unexplainable joy
to our hearts
Fills our souls with a peace
that passes understanding?
What captures the very essence
of heavenly Father's divine nature?
Loving!
It gives strength
to our physical bodies; to overcome
insurmountable odds;
It overrides all logic;
when the one it loves is in "harms way".
There is nothing that converts more,
heals quicker, uplifts greater;
Or defies the "laws of the physical realm"
more often than this singular act!
Thank you, heavenly Father,
for creating within us the "means" to
accomplish all things.
For eternal motivation and the ultimate
example Divine !!
Thank you, Lord, for making unending bliss mine.
Let us aspire to be touched by thy hand without end.

LOSS

When we lose the one we love---
Whether through death, a change in attitudes towards one another.
Or just plain contention with each other.
We are immediately faced with "a fork in the road".
On the one path we are confronted with seeking God's help with the matter and counting our many blessings shared with this person.
And giving thanks for the time we had together.
Believing that even though we are no longer physically together that heavenly Father will care for--
And take care of our loved one. Often times the hardest action for us to take is "standing still...and seeing God's Salvation". While standing still we may want to thank Him for His care and concern for our loss. Also for the peace He gives us; when we trust Him in all things. This might be a good time to remember that all we have is a gift from our heavenly Father.
Therefore which will we choose; the gift or the Giver!!
The other path is the path of contention with God. In taking this path we are doomed to bit by bit lose all the precious moments together; due to bitterness and a gradual "cooling of the heart". Thereby becoming overwhelmed with the loss --- forgetting the person and becoming entangled in constant grief.
Thus your loss becomes twofold; one the physical departure of your loved one. And two the slow but steady decline of your spiritual being. How quickly we can become a slave to despair and hopelessness. Loss definitely requires us to live the life of faith and hope eternal.
Or exposes us for our lack of trust in heavenly Father and His infinite wisdom. For if we trust Him; we do so completely---believing the object of His will is our eternal happiness. Also believing only He knows what is required   for us to fulfill our ultimate potential. If we seek His hand in all things; we will find it busy at work in our perfecting.

What a comfort to know that the One who framed the heavens and earth cares so for us that He spends His energies on our behalf. We should always remember that life is change. And new birth cannot manifest itself without "loss". Loss brings change and thereby life. It's our choice whether that change is a plus or a negative. Count your many blessings. Seek His face and presence and He will satisfy your mind and heart. I say this to you in the name of Jesus Christ; our Redeemer. Amen.

KNOWLEDGE

How excellent it is to know I have an eternal Father who
lives in heaven.
Who loves me and cares what happens in my life.
Whose constant desire is to help me live my life
in a way that will enable me to return to His presence.
A Father who nourishes me and strengthens me
in every manner that enables me to return to Him.
Whose love for me is perfect; and desires my
love for Him be perfect.
In accomplishing this perfection
He gives me each day and those persons and
challenges I require to obtain exaltation!
What a marvelous work He performs in me daily ---
if I will just humble myself and realize that all
I am and have come from Him; that I may know Him.
"Therefore, seek ye the giver and not the gift only.
... Seek ye first the kingdom of heaven and all things
will be added unto you."
For knoweth not our Father in heaven
our every need and desire?
Therefore, will He not strengthen us
that we may accomplish every perfect thing?
I am so glad to understand more and more each day---
how well heavenly Father understands exactly
what we need; that He may mold us into His perfect work;
that all men may see Him in each of us.

The Seedling

Inside each of us lies a still small part of God—
A seedling, if you will   This part of our being was a gift;
from a loving heavenly Father   To remind us
And keep us eternally "connected" to Him and He to us
We each must decide the "fate" of this precious gift
Shall we nourish nurture and encourage it
With love and beauty?
Or shall we neglect it
and forsake it
for external gain?
What shall its'
fate be;
Life eternal
In Light
and glory
Or the cold
blackness
of
separation
from God;
Its' author
and creator
Please contemplate
well its fate
For this decision
has eternal consequences.

December 2011

The love of our heavenly Father shows us Who we are... we are vessels of Love; His spirit children...with all the attributes of "Him"; within our being. We have the potential for compassion, love unfeigned, humility, hope eternal, patience, abounding forgiveness... all that our Father is... is right in our grasp... and yet not. What keeps us from enjoying life, from becoming His glory and most marvelous "work"? What are our "obstacles" to perfection? How has mortality, in its momentary /temporary status caused us to forget the One Who is All we shall ever need? It seems, with all our knowledge and intellect, it is challenging to remember, remember the foundation of all that we are and have and experience... briefly stated I imagine it is pride and arrogance that would avert us from heaven's gate. This time of the year we are again reminded the "reason for Life itself" ... and the greatest Gift, Ever!!!. Love, love, love.... Our Father in heavens love for us; His children... our Savior's love for His Father and us; His brothers and sisters... and our love for Them.... our Only Hope; in this life and the life to come. As we celebrate this season, let us venture beyond the temporary... past mediocrity and the "path often traveled" ... to the straight and narrow path; the one less traveled. Let us make a more tangible effort to accomplish the "greatest commandment" .... That we love the Lord our God; with All our heart, might, mind and strength.... And express that Love as we cherish our neighbor as ourselves. Herein lies Life Eternal.... That we acknowledge the hand of Him who created and Loved us first; our Father in heaven... even Elohim and His beloved Son Jesus Christ; our Savior. May this year be the beginning of unyielding Hope, determination and solace that No Matter What life brings we will choose Love overall and in all we do. That we will not allow disappointment, tragedy, failure, joy, success, anyone or thing keep us from our place at Father's side. I know God; the eternal Father lives, as does His Son; Jesus Christ that we are loved beyond are most exquisite imaginings. When we hear the words "Merry Christmas, may our hearts fill with the joy of this love; the love of Him Who has given His perfect Gift of eternity; for us and all those we hold dear. And I say these things, in the sacred name of Jesus Christ.

HE IS

He is what gives me life
He is my breath; the air that fills my lungs;
my very being; my joy; my reason for living.
There is no other who can comfort or give
peace or tranquility as He can
*For He is **the only One who has never failed me!***
In Him I can place all my fears; hopes and trust---
Without reservation.
For His eternal purpose is to bring to pass my
perfection. He is my soul's delight;
What makes my heart sing and my entire being
ache to please Him
For in so doing there can be only happiness
and true fulfillment --- eternally!
He is my soul's salvation
None other is capable or worthy enough to
accomplish my immortal pleasure
He is my sunshine; my rainbow; my pot of gold;
my morning song and midday delight
He brings joy in dry places
Love into darkness and despair
He is the One whom I shall praise all the days
of my life and for all time and eternity !!!

PREPAREDNESS

Therefore who shall receive oil to fill their lamps?
And how shall this filling be accomplished?
For those who are wise it will be in seeking
first the kingdom of God; In knowing it is our
Father's good pleasure to give us the kingdom;
In understanding the plan of salvation;
In loving and serving one another;
In enduring the trials and tribulations
that increase our faith and strengthen our relationship
with heavenly Father, Jesus Christ and the Holy Ghost.
In sharing our testimony of the truthfulness
of the Gospel and the Church.
In keeping the commandments and covenants
we have made --- thereby showing our love for
heavenly Father and acceptance of His will for our lives.
If we do these things our lives will exhibit
the fruit of the Spirit and our lamps shall be filled
That we may be as the wise virgins---
who were prepared to meet the bridegroom
and went in to the marriage feast.

Ebb

There is a place in the universe Where all waters
flow together at one great crook
In this ebb is contained the key to eternal
correctness for these waters Man with his devices
has polluted that which Father has given
And in so doing has altered the course of life
There are those who are One with this knowledge
and are from the corners of the universe
They, in their union can once again make whole
that which has been touched by the hand of ruin
If they would allow themselves to hear the voice
of the centuries And unite once again with
their Creator the damage can and will be reversed
This single union will right all previous wrongs
Erase the presence of current forces
And make One with the Father that which is His
He will once again be their Master And them
His children for all time and eternity.
In this moment we will all once again touch the
One who sent us here and know Him And be known by Him;
All previous dimness shall be expunged.
And we shall truly see Him face to face.

ADVERSARY

*He would have you **abandon** all that is decent,*
whole and uplifting
To forsake yourself in reckless abandonment
To over indulge in forbidden desires and thoughts
To experience that which he says is sweet and satisfying; But in
reality, leads to decay, destruction and total gradual
loss of control and ultimately stability. he would have you become
intimate friends
with misery and despair, he would have you believe
"You can have something for nothing"
That you are entitled to the maximum reward
for the least amount of effort That what you feel when you do wrong
is not regret (to be avoided)
But is power (to be sought over and over again).
he would have you caught in a never-ending circle of
defeat Rob you of your God given right of choice;
Absorb all that is glorious and good in you and return it
with the decay of corruption. he would steal slowly; but surely your
everlasting soul under the guise of friendship or companionship!!!
Beware of this "wolf in sheep's clothing" ---
His intent is unholy, unclean and the end thereof is
internship with him
For all time and eternity; you will remember
the error of your ways Be forever mindful of paths untaken;
repentance deserted
And the one who has encouraged this rebellion shall have
great joy in your demise.

UNKNOWN

*So many of us live in fear of that which we
cannot touch or taste or hear or see
We limit our whole existence here to our physicalness.
It's much "easier" to acknowledge only that which the
<u>mind</u> can embrace.
Even though we are continually urged by things unseen
to question that which our senses cannot solidify.
To delve into the essence of our true nature and being
To reach out and embrace the
"**unknown**" which merely **seems** unfamiliar to us
But in reality is the core of us.
This "unknown" we are fearful of and must be constantly
coaxed to embrace -- to seek
Is our heavenly Father and our pre-mortal existence
The love we came from-- It's what we all subconsciously
strive for day after day.
 But can only complete when we seek first the Creator---
He who sent us; He who loves us eternally.
Do not allow fear and trumped-up inhibitions to keep you
from discovering your true "roots".*

Try Jesus

When the storms
of life are raging all around
When it seems as though the
Sun will never shine again
Try Jesus for He is
Our Redeemer
Only in Him can
we find
the
"eye"
Of
The
storm

Lucifer

he is the one who besets all that is pure and
uncorrupted
Who twists, maims and compromises that
which was
once unadulterated. He was from the
beginning
The one who sought to place himself
Above Elohim; the Almighty Creator
and thereby
sinned from the beginning.
he is the
one who opposes
heavenly Father's
Work on every hand;
Who perverts the very scriptures
to his own behalf; Who uses half truths
and adulterated lies to obtain his means
Therefore.... BEWARE....
Least you find yourself
In his snare
Caught up
In a web
Of deceit
And entangles
In sin's grasp for all time and eternity

Christmas 2009

This is the time of the year we celebrate; in love... family. First, our Father in heaven and His Son, Jesus Christ (the first "gift" of Christmas).... Next, our own families and then our brothers and sisters across the globe (for we are all God's Family). The most valuable gift each of us possesses is our family....and the possibility to extend sincere love for each member. Whether families are large, small, connected by genetics or blood.... Or connected by just love... we are fortunate to be a part of something larger than ourselves. Although we may not fully appreciate the family's diversity ... within lies the opportunity to serve one another. It is in the family we develop the assurance of self-mastery... we discover how to uplift and support each other. We come to welcome our "humanness" and the fallacy thereof.... We learn to forgive and have compassion, one to another. The family environment is our initial "tutoring" in developing fruits of the Spirit; if we would look to Christ... the "author and finisher of our faith". As we develop in Christ like feelings for each other, we learn to pray often... to forgive daily... to speak the truth; in Love... to open ourselves to all that God has to offer us. His desire is for us to find joy in our light; for it is eternal.... We diminish, as we abide in "darkness" which is ever so near... with its fleeting pleasures. Let us not be as the world; crude and ever yielding to that which is a base. Therefore, let us strive to live a life of gratitude; by finding and developing the best in ourselves and others. Let us not fear our inner Light (the Light of Christ within) but seek after it and once found, thrive therein. The scriptures tell us "Let your light so shine, that men may see your good works and glorify your Father in heaven". May we "glorify our heavenly Father" as we express our gratitude for His gift of His only begotten Son; our Lord and Savior; the Prince of Peace; Wonderful; Counselor; Almighty God; the Everlasting Father... even Jesus Christ. May we love Him so much that we too willing to give away all our sins to "know Him"; as we are known of Him. Then shall the "babe" who forsook heaven to dwell here below... smile upon each of us; for our "works" shall be pleasing and eternally saving... us and our kindred. These things I say humbly; in the name of Jesus Christ. Amen.

PRAISE

Thank you, for holding me in your arms and warming this body; When the pressures in this life have chilled me to the bone And I indeed feel the coldness of being a stranger in a strange land. Thank you, for lifting my head from my pillow after Mom died and all I desired was to sleep forever. I am glad you picked me up and carried me to work — That my mind and body might busy itself with service.... And, heal. I cannot count the times you've held my hand and led me to the next step.... What a frightening place we live in; If you are not near. May I always remember You and the service You give me; hourly! And may I express my appreciation by returning that service to others. No matter who they are or where they are going. Let me not judge; For only You can guide a path and know the end thereof. Help me, dear Father, acknowledge Thee in all things. And therein obtain true, eternal balance in my life

ℑ

I Am the Lord; thy God
The King of kings
The bread of Life; thy
rod, thy staff --- The Creator
of all things
I Am the Way; the Truth
and the Life
There is none above me
No other knows thee altogether
I Am alpha and omega--- thy beginning
-- The Author and finisher of thy faith.
The one who calls thee to a higher
mark and existence.
I Am LOVE
and have created thee in love,
And desire that you return
to your glorious beginnings
And that you become whole as I Am Whole.
That we may once again be ONE.
I Am all you need to accomplish the full
measure of your creation---
IT IS MY EARNEST DESIRE!
As it was in the beginning so let it be
accomplished. In the name of my Only begotten,
Jesus Christ. Amen.

THE GIFT

This year has been a year of miracles…. For moments at a time we have become One in purpose- Affording us a glimpse of our pre-mortal existence It has been marvelous to see us lay aside our differences And focus on those things we know to be true and divine. Disaster after disaster we have reached out to each other in brotherly love …. Disregarding race, national origin or religion… We have seen hearts mended; age old prejudices challenged and conquered- Thus being reminded we all are God's Children and accountable to Him; our Creator….. We have seen history rewritten/ redressed in a manner unimaginable just a generation ago…. This day is a day of jubilee; for God's words are being fulfilled speedily and His revelations constant …. "all that has been done in the dark shall be made known" For those who love the Lord and are called according to His purposes should have a glad heart…. Great joy and renewed determination to endure all our Father sees fit to bless us with….. The season of harvest is upon us… A time to cleave even stronger to that we know to be correct…. To act upon the prompting of the Holy Ghost; the first time- knowing the voice of whom we serve….. having developed a more sure knowledge of His will…. And walking therein This day the intense refiner's fire dissipates the former dross of fear, of hopelessness, of shame, of that which would decrease the Light of Christ within each of us…. I am encouraged that we as a people (God's people) are more marvelous than we know And are closer to perfection that we imagine. More and more we are beginning to understand we don't have to prove our beauty and worth as the world sees these things… but as God, the Eternal Father sees… Knowing for the first time true freedom. Freedom from the chains of darkness and eternal misery As the angels sang so joyously long ago; on the night of the new star- the Light of the world arose…. Glory to God, glory to God; peace on earth good will toward men… For unto us a child is born… and His name shall be called Wonderful, Counselor, Almighty God, The Everlasting Father The Prince of Peace May we remember the first Gift of Christmas; our Lord and Savior, Jesus Christ and bring Him our hearts and willingness to serve and uplift one another…. For by this shall men know… We are His- that we love one another; as He Loves us And be determined to follow our Lord and Savior in thought, word and deed… therein presenting to Him a gift not only "clean" on the outside but on the inside also. Let us give the one gift that is pleasing and acceptable to He who knows and sees All…. Our hearts, minds and wills. In so doing we will experience the greatest Christmas and gift of all ---- a new birth … having our hearts filled with much charity for Him and all mankind.

Christmas 2008

Thanksgiving '96

Thanksgiving comes at least three times a day;
In the morning when I rise and thank God for
life and a new start
At noon as I reflect upon matters of the heart
And again at eve, as I'm driving in my car---
I compare notes with heavenly Father...
To see if I've done my part
For the Bible says "... but be filled with the Spirit,
speaking to yourselves in psalms and hymns
and spiritual songs, singing and making melody
in your heart to the Lord, Giving thanks always
for all things unto God and the Father in the
name of our Lord Jesus Christ" (Eph. 5:18l -20)
Therefore, if thanksgiving does not come at
least three times each day for everyone of us
What shall we have to celebrate on the fourth
Thursday in November...
If we have not taken the time, in days past to
acknowledge Him each step of the way?
Isn't Thanksgiving really a daily song of the heart?
And the fourth Thursday in November
merely the opportunity to share that song with
.... The world?

I Forgot

Today I gave in to sin and allowed myself an indiscretion I indulged in that which is unseemly in God's sight; That which He cannot look upon; even in the smallest degree I neglected to entreat the Comforter; who has been given for this specific purpose--- to remind me of Who I am; and of my worth – as a child of the Most High Whose Son gave His life; that I should not have to suffer these things --- For He bore ALL on my behalf For a moment I forgot that true satisfaction can only co me through obedience to the laws of life I forgot that there is nothing in our realm of existence that our Savior has not known; for us. I forgot He tasted the bitterness of self-hate; of inadequacy; of loathing; of all manner of ungodliness --- for me. I forgot He loved me so much He suffered ALL; that He may effectively comfort and guide me; in my trials. He willingly took these upon Himself; That I might be free--- And would not "know" this bitter, desolate road I now travel. For a moment I forgot His love divine; that is my only eternal joy; I forgot to seek heavenly Father's truth and knowledge – which He promised He would give "those who diligently sought it". I forgot the dominion He gave me over the works of His hands. And, to call upon the name of Jesus; that I may be delivered from this place wherein I stand. It is my earnest prayer to learn this lesson well; That this toad will not be re -traveled by me. That I will more literally "remember my Lord and Savior; And take His name upon me" in all things That I may run this rave to the end. Remembering He has not forgotten me --- but remembers me always; And delivers me continually.

DAUGHTER

I am a daughter of God !!!!!!!!
Sent here to find joy in the measure of my creation
To experience for myself the "more abundant life" promised ... By
my Lord and Savior... And to
experience the peace and joy unspeakable that comes from living
the Gospel of Jesus Christ. When I keep
the commandments heavenly Father gives me the power of living in
the light of truth--- Which is indeed
liberating in every way. When I seek the truth of all
things and am lead by the Holy Spirit I am empowered with wisdom
and knowledge from on high
As I live my life in accordance to the Gospel I
experience spiritual growth and become closer to my Father in
heaven I began to realize with each step of obedience His marvelous
plan of salvation for my life.
I find comfort and peace in being chaste, loving and upright before
the Lord. I am pleased to have this opportunity to come here and
experience and live a life
of service to others ---- And thereby walk in my
Savior's footsteps. For is so doing I am awakened
inside to who my heavenly Father intended me to be.
How excellent His love is for me!! What a marvelous
God I serve And what divine destinations He has awaiting me ----
Therefore I shall take great pleasure in living every "line and
precept" of the Gospel;
for therein is my true "nature" developed. And with help from my
heavenly Father all power shall be remitted unto me... That I may
fill the exact measure of my creation.

BOYCHILD

I am a son of God; Therein is my strength; my greatest worth and ultimate potential. There is no other title; position or calling which possess more prestige than this! My being expands all time And my authority almighty; for my heavenly Father gives all power unto my hands; as I become worthy and capable of handling it. Because I respect and honor this gift of God; I shall not attempt to use it to enslave; subdue or undermine others. I shall not use the prowess I've been given to demean or subject others to my will. Instead I shall use all my being to learn to love; encourage, support and lift others .... Because I am person enough to do so without feeling threatened. And also because those things that I share with others multiply themselves back unto my being. That which is weak and petty diminishes; as I "seek first the kingdom of God"--- For in His light these things cannot survive! As heavenly Father's son I am heir to all He has. Therefore I have no need to covet that which belongs to another. My strength comes from the support of my family and living the Gospel. My worth from that which I share with those around me. Each day I learn how to rightly divide the Word of God and am thereby strengthened eternally. My greatest potential is in my desire to find joy in fulfilling the measure of my creation And becoming what Father is ....LOVE. May I continually employ all that I am to meet this end.

FE/MALE

Male/female are one with each other
Not in competition; but in singularity with
God
and the natural flow and order of things. Not
contending, one against the other but in perfect
harmony;
Oneness with each other
Each has a part the other requires for completion;
Oneness with He who sent them!
Be at peace; One with another and therein
experience God; the Creator and Master
of all.

DEFICIT

These days things are valid
Or have worth Only if they can fit on a ledger page
Or can be labeled as a *credit* or *debt.*
It would appear nothing has "value" if it does
not fall into accountable columns.
If it doesn't fit into a package of one sort or the
other---- it's valueless; void of meaning and not worth time or
attention.
And as persistent as most of us are; too often we seem to end up
on the *minus* side!!!
 But be of good cheer ---
For the final count has not been taken
That count whose results are of eternal consequence. The final
accounting of our status while here can only
be taken by the ultimate Judge; the judge of **all Judges**--- Whose
rulings are final indeed.
He is the bridegroom and the value He seeks is in the
preparedness of His people;
The amount of oil in their lanterns.
Only then can the books be truly balanced.
In that moment the "first shall be last; and the last first" And those
who may seem lacking in this realm may have their lanterns full;
prepared to meet the bridegroom and sup with Him.
For this oil is more precious than fine silver or gold
And more desirable than the largest gemstone.
There is no substitute for our spiritual preparedness. None other
can prepare for the *final balancing of the books* but you.
Therefore, we should most surely "be about our Father's
business". For only therein shall we be found on the *plus* side of
the time and eternity column.

COMPROMISE

It's what you do when you are afraid
to step up to the plate and swing –for fear you
might strike out or appear foolish
in some way Or,
what you do when you listen to all the reasons
you cannot;
Instead of taking a chance that the
"flame" you have within shall burn on;
Even in the face of defeat.
Or, even worse what you do
because you feel unworthy or ill equipped to
handle the task before you. Compromise says I
don't have the confidence; The faith to follow the
road to happiness; Or fulfillment; or success; or
accomplishment It means I believe more in fear
than in a loving Creator whose desire is for me
to live "life more abundantly".

December 2010

So soon it is Christmas time once again, an opportunity for us to turn our thoughts and hearts to the first gift of Christmas.... Our Lord and Savior; Jesus Christ. The one who gave up the opulence of heaven... His seat at our heavenly Father's side... to demonstrate His love for us; His brothers and sisters. He came that we might comprehend loves true and sincere expression.... More than mere words... but action, dedication and devotion were required to meet the demands of justice. How precious are we to warrant such sacrifice and fidelity? And what can we give to demonstrate our appreciation and gratitude for such a treasure? Of time we are reminded in the scriptures of Father's desire for us... that we love one another; as He has loved us... more than words are needed for this to materialize. More than thoughts are required to "fulfill the measure of our creation". Each of us must commit ourselves daily to our brothers and sisters care and welfare.... That we might emulate our Savior's example.

May we too dedicate ourselves to lives of appreciation and gratitude. Appreciation of pure; unadulterated love divine... gratitude for eternity and the chance to express sincere courage and determination in striving to be true and faithful to the One who never forsakes us. What "gift" may we give to know Him who is aware of every molecule of our being.... Are we willing to give our pride, our anger, our hate, our rebellion? May we strive to forgive those who have despised us and continue our progression towards eternal Life. May we follow the admonition of Paul in that we will not allow anyone or thing to "separate us from the love of God; the eternal Father". This Christmas may we remember from whence we came.... Heaven... a sphere more grand and magnificent than we can imagine in this mortal state. And once we have remembered may we conduct ourselves as His blessed Sons and

Daughters. Therein may our Savior be lifted up; for all men to see and glorify God... as the angels did that first Christmas morn. May we each be the instruments of "Peace on earth; good will toward men" this season. In the name of our Lord and Savior Jesus Christ I pray. Amen

LIFE

I was reminded today of what a precious gift we have
A special endowment from our heavenly Father to us--- His children
The chance to experience joy, pain, laughter, sadness, love, misery,
exhilaration, pleasure, satisfaction, failure and much more in the
gambit of emotions brought on by this simple experience called "life".
I recalled the anxiousness of "separation" from heavenly Father on
the one hand
And the joy unspeakable of the opportunity to know;
first-hand what living is. With all the ups and downs
Yes these are adventures to be had. And tho' there is oft
unpleasantness--- pain—grief
These are not the totality of our sojourn here. They are mere
"pebbles" --- Granted pebbles that sometimes seem to continually
manifest themselves
But pebbles none the less! The sum total of our existence here is as
we perceive it.
A matter of attitude; either joyous for the most part; balanced with
moments of grief
Or grievous with few moments of joy or pleasure.
The outlook is ours --- What shall the view be?
Worth living to the fullest or undesirable?
Joyous or painful? The choice is ours. For some of us life is an
awesome adventure to be had--- With each day being one of eager
anticipation
Like a child, eternally experiencing growth; moment by moment.
Hardly ever remembering the pain of failure or disappointment
But forever looking forward; moving onward--- stretching upward
for our every step
With each step being new and breathtaking; filled with anticipation
and joy.
As a new day dawning or a color drenched sunset; divinely beautiful.
And forever reminding us of our heavenly Father's tremendous love
for us

Why Am I?

So, why am I here; If not to love
And how can I love Unless I reach out to my fellow man and
touch the face of God--- For He Is Love
How can I touch His face
Except I diligently seek Him and learn of Him ?
In seeking Him I "peer" into His mirror
And slowly; orderly I learn the "taste", the "feel"---
The very essence of love
As I come to "see" the One who gave His time; energy;
thoughts; desires--- His very life for me
My being begins to understand what love is.
For it is so much more than words; it is words made manifest!!!!
So why am I here ?
I am here to learn how to love and to accept love;
To come to know and appreciate the balance in all things; To
take the smallest and weakest part of me and develop it. To
share that which heavenly Father has given me freely; that the
whole may be edified; To see alone I can only fail---
But in Father I can do all things; according to His will
I am here to recall my glorious beginning
And my limitless possibilities
To learn how to live in my God given freedom;
instead of allowing fear and greed to rob me of my birthright.
Simply put, I am here because heavenly Father
loves me and knows me altogether
And desires that I come to know Him; Altogether---
And thus become one with He who sent me.

DARE

Dare
to be
sons and
daughters of
our heavenly Father
Dare to be fed by His almighty
Word--- Whether through revelation,
scripture or prophet---Let Him be heard
Dare to rise above this earthly mire
And make our Father's will your desire
Dare to be faithful, just and true
And to accomplish all that
Father sent you here to do
Dare to submit your thoughts
means and desires that
Father may be
glorified through and in them
And you shall
be molded
by a
heavenly
fire
Dare to be all Father
would have you to be
**Then exaltation
you shall see!!**

LOVE

For eons I have sat at your feet
Since there was where I found security; purpose and knowledge
When there you told me of your life and experiences;
Of the lessons you learned and the pain of failure
As I sat time after time with eyes closed; to embrace all around me.
I experienced the sound of your voice, majestic yet so comforting;
I sensed every part of you.
My taste was overwhelmed with the sweetness of you;
My smell with your fragrance;
My touch with the pleasure of your very being;
My entire creation was a part of you!
And then the day came for us to part---
What joy; knowing that on my return
we would have grown closer.
So thus was my preexistence with you...
Now I must learn to recapture those solemn,
quite moments at your feet
Learn once again to wait on every word you say;
Learn to know the essence of you again---
Remember how we became ONE.
I know that with your help I shall accomplish all you
have sent me to do;
That I will touch those you sent me to touch
Experience that which I must for your glory
For you have told me of these things
and prepared me to overcome that which requires conquering;
And absorb that which is of US.
May I travel this road well that when
I return we may once again embrace for all time and eternity.
Thank you, my eternal friend, Lord, Father ---- Creator.

Thanksgiving '97

Thanksgiving is what you do
As you begin to appreciate the atonement
and its implications in your life.
Action requires action.
You offer gratitude and service to
our eternal heavenly Father.

Thanksgiving keeps you humble
And ever mindful of Father's constant care
It enables your vision; thoughts and actions
to be used of God.
Because your heart's desire is to please the
one who gives thanks for us.

For every parent is grateful for each
gift of love they receive in their children.
And our heavenly Father is no exception---
He set the guidelines.

Mortality

Mortality is short.
We have only a moment to be a friend;
sister, brother, father, mother, son,
daughter, wife, husband, aunt, uncle,
employee/employer ...
a moment to Be/.... exist
A few seconds to enjoy the fruits thereof
And perhaps – if we are loving
enough; eternity to share....
Together with those we have come to care for, support,
encourage and express
true emotion
- Together in pure love we; through the
unadulterated sacrifice of our Redeemer, - are made whole;
complete;
without lack or want Only together can we
become All we were meant to Be Together will we
"no longer be strangers" ...but called
Friends, heirs and joint heirs with our Savior, King, Lord,
Prince... our only Hope; even Jesus

BEING

There is a wholeness;
A completeness that comes
with mere purpose in our existence.
The veil is parted moment by moment
And we are allowed a brief remembrance
Times wherein our heavenly Father's presence
surrounds us with an embrace of unspeakable warmth.
As we diligently seek His face He gives us instances
of oneness with Him.
Occurrences of premortal bliss.
Our bodies are then caught up in Him and
reminded of total surrender --confidence--
"apartness" -- being one with the universe.
We must seek these moments oft.
As they are the meat of our purpose here.
This is the eternal remembrance we must complete
In order to once again live with our heavenly Father.
It's there; but we must call upon Him ---
His purpose for our being
To find the road home.
Seek the straight and narrow---
it is the walk you are meant to fulfill---
the ultimate measure of your creation.

JOHN

I sat at heavenly Father's feet and absorbed His every word and action.

We loved and respected each other in a manner few have experienced;

Besides my cousin --- The Only Begotten of the Father. When the plan of salvation was presented, pure joy filled my being   And the opportunity to be a part of that plan; by giving service extraordinary was unspeakably wondrous.   Soon the time came for me to receive a mortal body- It had begun!!

I was to be my Lord and Master's forerunner--- "The voice of one crying in the wilderness, "Prepare ye the way of the Lord..." I was conceived by Elisabeth; in her old age Manifesting there is nothing too great for God to accomplish and His promises are true.   The hand of God was with me from the beginning.   I was chosen from the beginning and it was well with me. I lived a life of obedience to my Lord and sealed my testimony of His divinity with my death.   I was prepared diligently in the preexistence for this cause. I was lectured and taught the Word; that there may not be any lack in my testimony and service; For I was to prepare the world for the arrival of the Lamb of God. So great was my desire to serve my Master that even before my birth I leaped in my mother's womb at the very closeness of Him!   It was my joy to give knowledge of salvation and repentance to people.

The most glorious day of my life was the day I; having been given the keys of baptism by heavenly Father; baptized my Lord and Savior, Jesus Christ.   And for a moment that seemed to pass all time and eternity I experienced heavenly Father's great pleasure in the obedience of His Son and the service given by me.   That pleasure was shown through the manifestation of the Holy Spirit in the form of a dove

And through His audible voice from heaven saying "This is my beloved Son, in whom I am well pleased".

My faith was renewed and my testimony enlarged that day.   And, at that precise moment I recalled Father's words "... I will put my laws into their mind; and write them in their hearts; and I will be to them a God; and they shall be to me a people". These words were reaffirmed in my heart and witnessed by heavenly Father and the Holy Ghost.

How excellent to serve the One and Only Living God and to be a part of His divine plan of salvation. And what profit to seal that testimony with my last breath!!!!

Member

I am a member of the Body of Christ
I am not alone; there are innumerable members of this body All are
heavenly Father's;
All were called by Him--- to be His; To hear His voice and
obey His will.
All are here for one end result; To remember to learn to live as One
As the Father, the Son and the Holy Ghost are One
And as we once were with Them.
There are those who have gone before me and
those who will follow me
But each of us is specific; in our existence and purpose We each
possess a unique love; given to touch
in a special way---- AS ONLY WE CAN.
And so Father has called us to perform that which only we can. As
our Savior before us gave what
ONLY HE COULD GIVE our eternal salvation; and the right back to
heavenly Father's presence.
Let us therefore, not lose our focus
Or become so entangled in this mortal existence that we forget our
immortal beginnings;
And thence neglect our only meaningful reason for being here ---
Obtaining eternal life with our heavenly Father!!
There is nothing more
fulfilling, satisfying or exhilarating than spending all time and
*eternity with the one who **personifies** LOVE*

Victory in Christ

There are no victims in Christ; only victories as we
look to Him in all
You've been beaten and robbed, left for dead by the
wayside?
A stranger comes to your side who was your enemy
And binds up your wounds, carries you to safety and
ensures a place to heal- victory
You've been caught in sin, condemned to death?
A friend picks you up and pleads your case til
the accusers flee- victory
You lost your family, home, and friends;
but not your hope and faith in Christ - victory
From prison Paul has taught us "count it all joy when
Diverse times come upon you; knowing that the trying
of your faith worketh patience.
But let patience have her perfect work, that ye maybe
perfect and entire, wanting nothing"-
victory in Christ Our only hope and salvation
forever and ever.
Amen

Girlchild

I am a child of God!   Sent here to "fulfill the measure
of my creation"   And how shall it be accomplished,
unless Father shows me the way?
And how can He show me 'cept I learn to listen
And obey? Father has given me many blessings;
Some which are easily seen and all in need of development
One of my blessings is beauty;   Not as the world views beauty
But the eternal kind; the one that comes from within
So no matter what my external appearance internally
I radiate the "fruits of the Spirit".
For the world judge's beauty by corruptible standards;
True beauty is incorruptible and eternal. Another of my gifts is love;
the ability to see beyond one's faults and fill his needs.

To nourish, encourage, support and nurture those around me
Whether they acknowledge me or not; because it brings me joy!!

Knowing that One who sees in private rewards openly those who
diligently seek Him.

Because Father has blessed me with these gifts I must treasure them
and keep them sacred   That I may reap the benefits of righteous
living---Blessings untold from my Father in heaven. For what parent
does not desire to endow their child with happiness, fulfillment and
love? What Father desires not his child to be nigh unto him and he
to them? For this cause I must always remember who I am.

And not surrender to anyone or thing less than the perfect
Love of God.

And that love can only be found in one place ---- in Him our heavenly
Father. Therefore He shall head my life and all those
I surround myself with

For I AM a daughter of God-- A child of Light and beauty And therein
can have no part in darkness!!!